Made
for the
Mountains

Made for the Mountains

BO BAKER

Word Books, Publisher
Waco, Texas

MADE FOR THE MOUNTAINS

Copyright © 1977 by Word Incorporated, Waco, Texas.
All rights reserved. No part of this book may be reproduced in any form, except for brief quotations in reviews, without the written permission of the publisher.

All Scripture quotations, unless otherwise noted, are from the King James Version of the Bible.

The quotation marked Phillips is from *The New Testament in Modern English,* copyright © J. B. Phillips 1958, 1960, 1972.

Grateful acknowledgment is made for the use of the following copyrighted material:

"Aurora Leigh," by Elizabeth Barrett Browning. Reprinted from *The Treasury of Religious Verse* edited by Donald T. Kauffman. Copyright © 1962 by Fleming H. Revell Company, and used by permission.

Quotation from *Men As Trees Walking* by Margaret T. Applegarth. Copyright © 1952 by Harper and Row, Publishers, Inc., and used by permission.

"Can Man Survive?" by James A. Oliver. Copyright © 1970 *American Way,* inflight magazine of American Airlines. Reprinted by permission.

"July 6, 1961," from *Markings* by Dag Hammarskjöld, translated by Leif Sjoberg and W. H. Auden, copyright © 1965 by Alfred A. Knopf, Inc., and used by permission.

"Renascence," from *Collected Poems,* Harper and Row. Copyright 1917, 1945, by Edna St. Vincent Millay and Norma Millay Ellis.

"I Will Have My Dream," by BO Baker, copyright © 1977 by Crescendo Music Publications, Inc., and reprinted by permission.

"Come, Rest Awhile," by BO Baker, copyright © 1972 by Crescendo Music Publications, Inc., and reprinted by permission.

"His Way—Mine!" by BO Baker, copyright © 1971 by Crescendo Music Publications, Inc., and reprinted by permission.

"Teach Me to Care," by BO Baker, copyright © 1971 by Crescendo Music Publications, Inc., and reprinted by permission.

All poetry not otherwise credited is the work of the author.

The author and publisher have sought unsuccessfully to locate source information for the quotation of "The Divine Tragedy" by St. John Adcock. If such information is made available to us, full credit will be given in future editions.

ISBN 0-87680-504-7
Library of Congress catalog card number: 76-48503
Printed in the United States of America

To

Dick
David
Lisa Carol

With love

Contents

	Foreword	11
	Preface	13
1	The Borrowed Glow	15
2	An Attitude for Attainment	22
3	Made for the Mountains	32
4	A Disposable Religion	41
5	Come Rest Awhile	48
6	The Lesson of the Lake	57
7	A Handle to Fit My Hand	66
8	The Unrecognized Christ	74

Foreword

This volume of Christian messages entitled *Made for the Mountains* is worthy of the careful reading on the part of every Christian everywhere. If we give the book to those who are lost, it is my earnest persuasion that it will be blessed by the Holy Spirit to the conversion of souls.

Most of the sermons printed in this volume have been preached in our First Baptist Church in Dallas, either while BO Baker served as our interim pastor while I was away in the summertime, when he was preaching a revival meeting before our congregation, or while he has filled the pulpit on other occasions.

Dr. George W. Truett was my predecessor in the pastorate of the First Baptist Church in Dallas. During the forty-seven years he ministered to these dear people, one of the sermons that he delivered was entitled "The Need for Encouragement." This book by BO Baker is a continuation of that marvelous theme. No greater message could one hear from heaven than that of the loving presence and tender care of our Lord.

For several years now BO Baker has been pastor of the strategic and growing Plymouth Park Baptist Church of Irving Texas, a suburb of the metropolitan area of Dallas. God has blessed him greatly in his shepherdly care of that church. You will see and you will feel this hand of God upon the preacher as you read the chapters of the book.

Let me say a word of personal love and esteem for BO Baker. He gladdens my heart every time I see him, and he blesses my soul every time I hear him. What he has meant to me in this personal friendship, he will mean to you wherever you are when you read of God's goodness through the pages of this book.

W. A. CRISWELL
Pastor, First Baptist Church
Dallas, Texas

Preface

My heart tells me that all of us need encouragement. These messages are meant to brighten the way and lighten the load. It is not always easy to be loyal to royal things. Sometimes it is even difficult to find the way. Although we are "Made for the Mountains" most of us are more familiar with the valley walk.

Should there be those who read these lines and come to love the Lord more dearly, to walk his way more surely, to share his truth more freely—then, it will have been worth it all.

For my wife, Tina, whose walk with me through the years has encouraged this writing, I am truly grateful. She shares with me in every line.

I am indebted to Mrs. Maxine Off, my capable secretary, for preparing the manuscript, and to a dedicated staff for making possible the time necessary for preparation.

These messages have been joyfully proclaimed across this land and beyond. I have watched the Spirit work wonders with God's Word and would not have missed it for the world!

B O BAKER

1

The Borrowed Glow

> Now Moses kept the flock of Jethro his father in law, the priest of Midian: and he led the flock to the backside of the desert, and came to the mountain of God, even to Horeb.
> And the angel of the Lord appeared unto him in a flame of fire out of the midst of a bush: and he looked, and, behold, the bush burned with fire, and the bush was not consumed.
> And Moses said, I will now turn aside, and see this great sight, why the bush is not burnt.
> And when the Lord saw that he turned aside to see, God called unto him out of the midst of the bush, and said, Moses, Moses. And he said, Here am I.
> And he said, Draw not nigh hither: put off thy shoes from off thy feet, for the place whereon thou standest is holy ground. Exodus 3:1-5

For those who would see and hear and feel deeply, there is a superlative truth within these lines. The experience of the man in God's back pasture was not meant to be exclusive. This immortal incident in the Midian Desert can happen wherever there is a man who will "turn aside to see."

We have had a tendency to allow this Bible presentation to gather dust in the back corner of this Old Testament book when, in reality, it has tremendous relevancy to today's life and living.

The thing that happened to Moses can happen today. Indeed, it does happen today! God is still in the burning bush business and needs only those who are ignitable as reason for a holy happening.

It is only fair to say that Moses had not always been a man of God. He knew the meaning of temper and of patience. His impetuousness in aiding a Hebrew brother had brought upon him the wrath of the Egyptian authorities. Because of this incident he had fled to a lonely hideaway deep in the Midian Desert. Moses knew that he was a wanted man, but he did not realize that the one who wanted him most was God. But for all this and in all this he was still God's man. He had been chosen for a specific and unique purpose. So, with the desert for his classroom and a thorn bush for a laboratory, God brought the man Moses face to face with life's indispensable—the will of God.

In the out-of-the-way place, the inconspicuous place, Moses came into confrontation with the deep things of the soul. Never had he felt so completely alone, unwanted and overlooked. Never had he felt so unlikely a candidate for divine appointment. Fortunately for him God had other plans. Here was one leading lambs to water whom God had chosen to lead a nation through the Red Sea. Here was one carrying a shepherd's staff who would wield it as a sacred scepter before the mightiest monarch of that day.

Although Moses was not aware of it, he was God's choice as the instrument for a nation's deliverance. All God needs to accomplish a mission or a work is one man or woman whose life is completely available to him.

It is not unusual for God to choose an unlikely man in an unlikely place for a royal service. Greatly used men and women are often those who have come to the limit of their own strength and ingenuity. This is as heaven intended it. It is only when one comes to realize his own total inadequacies that he is able to lean hard upon the adequacy of Christ.

Take Time for the Eternal

"In this day when one believes that happiness can be prescribed by physicians and dispensed by druggists—a day trying to fight its way to peace, buy its way to eternity, drink its way to pleasure and filibuster its case before God, the truth needs to be told in forthright clarity," says Roy O. McClain in his book *This Way Please*. The message of divine truth needs to be heard as never before: mankind, all mankind, needs a holy encounter with God!

We have become a people of scattered loyalties and, for the most part, a people preoccupied with trivialities. The lure of the shortcut has completely captivated the mind of most. Thousands bow before the shrine of discount discipleship. In the midst of "nine-day wonder plans" and minimasterpieces, there has come the impression that Christian discipleship is obtainable in a special paperback edition, and that spiritual power is available at wholesale prices.

This non-biblical delusion must be immediately dispelled. There are no shortcuts to discipleship! God has no light crosses for rent! Following Jesus is a serious business. Holy things are experienced by those who take time for the eternal. God reserves the sights and sounds of sacred things for those who take the time to wait and watch before him. If you have not experienced a divine encounter lately it may be that you have not taken time for one.

All of us need those moments when we stand in awe before some mighty work of God. It is good to have those times when we are enthralled and overwhelmed in his presence. There are far too few breathtaking moments these days, and our world is the poorer because of it.

A religion without its exclamation points is a religion

without the power to motivate. This presents no problem for the Christian, however, for the message of Christ is alive with exhilaration and challenge and spiritual intrigue. There has never been anything dull or drab about following Christ; and may heaven forgive us should we ever lose the thrill and excitement of being children of God!

Look for Your Burning Bush

Elizabeth Barrett Browning, with intuitive insight, penned these lines in her poem "Aurora Leigh":

> Earth's crammed with heaven,
> And every common bush afire with God;
> But only he who sees, takes off his shoes,
> The rest sit round it and pluck blackberries.

What a commentary on the experience of God's man in Midian!

We dare not presume that Moses was looking for "a bush afire with God." But it was to his credit that he did not miss it. God chose the instrumentality of a common desert bush to hold holy fire while he "caught" the attention of Moses. So often he chooses to use the ordinary, the unpretentious, the mundane, as instruments of divine revelation.

It is always a delight to observe the variety of things which God chooses to use as instruments in the leading and directing of his children.

He used dew-drenched fleece to reinforce his call to Gideon. He used hornets to prove his power over Israel's ancient enemies. He used a shepherd's staff to demonstrate his point to Pharaoh. He used a servant girl in Naaman's household to provide information leading to the healing of the leprous captain. He used a big fish to provide living quarters for Jonah until the runaway evangelist was right

The Borrowed Glow

for revival. He used all manner of things. He used broken pitchers, rams' horns, a slingshot and slender reeds. He used rain, roses, ravens, ox yokes and candlelight. He used thorns and nails and an ugly rough cross with his own son hanging on it; and, oh yes, he used a burning bush.

Are you listening? More than that are you looking for your "burning bush"? God may choose to speak through a song or a sermon. He may reveal his will through a friend, a family member, or a fellowship. Many testify of his divine revelation while in the dialogue of a prayer. Others insist that the light of his leadership came slowly as step by step they moved out to the very edge of all the faith they possessed and, in so doing, made the grand discovery.

What is your burning bush? I do not know. The answer can be found only in the mind and heart of God. To dogmatize at this point would be akin to the "miracle on demand" syndrome advocated by the scribes and Pharisees in Jesus' day (Matt. 12:38). It is not so important what method or means God chooses to use to reveal himself. It is important that one be spiritually alert and sensitive in recognizing the revelation when it comes. It is important also that one stand ready to receive it with a surrendered will.

How meaningful are the words, "And Moses said, I will now turn aside, and see . . ." (Exod. 3:3). Suppose he had failed to look. Suppose he had missed God's bush aglow. One can only contemplate the tragedy of such a loss. How often, how very often God's "burning bush" has been overlooked because of impatience, preoccupation, and worldly pressures.

May I ask again, have you looked for your burning bush?

Burning-bush experiences are never given to enjoy. They are given to establish responsibility, to inspire being, doing, and going.

Moses' responsibility before God led him from the hidden place to a magnificent palace of Pharaoh. What a contrast!

From a keeper of sheep to counselor of Kings. The same basic set of principles that gave meaning and purpose to the life of Moses gives meaning and purpose to the life of every committed Christian. He or she must stand ready for spiritual assignment or reassignment wherever the will of God may direct. The dedicated Christian is always on alert.

For more than a million Hebrew slaves, Moses became their "burning bush." He was God's chosen deliverer. He was God's revealer of truth. Through his inspiring influence and persuasive leadership a whole nation left Egypt for the Promised Land. It came about because one man in a lonely place caught sight of a bush that burned with fire and was not consumed.

It does not press Scripture beyond rationality nor truth beyond measure to conclude that God may have chosen you to so bear witness of his grace that you become his burning bush for someone else.

If God can take a twisted desert plant, set it on fire, and use it to speak to a discouraged Hebrew shepherd, he can surely ignite the life and testimony of a dedicated child of God and reveal himself to others through their borrowed glow. This is the imperative of the Christian life—to reflect the borrowed glow.

That glow is so beautifully illustrated in a story coming out of World War II. The world went to pieces for five years—from 1940 to 1945—and it was during this time that Martin Niemöller, a German pastor, was imprisoned by the Nazis for speaking out boldly for Christ and in defiance of the Führer. Because of his defiance of Hitler he was placed in solitary confinement and kept there for eight years. Separated from his loved ones and congregation, he sought earnestly for some method whereby he could become a useful servant of God. Finally he came upon an idea. Each day he moved his table under the high windows of his cell.

The Borrowed Glow

He then placed his chair on that table and climbed up on the chair to stand on tiptoe in order to get as close as possible to the grating of the window above his head. Then he waited for the strange sound of scuffling which would begin rising from the courtyard far below—that crunching of feet on gravel that told him now the other prisoners were out for their daily airing. At that very moment Pastor Niemöller began to whisper stirring passages from the Bible. This he did over and over, day by dragging day. He had no way of knowing that they heard, but the single fact that the scuffling sounds became less noisy on the gravel gave him reason to hope.

Through months of uncertainty he offered this mystical ministry, always in prayer that God would use even such an absentee instrument as a disembodied voice to awaken hope in the hopeless, faith in the faithless, love in the loveless. It is not surprising that on his release at the end of the war, Dorothy Thompson reported on the striking incandescence of his face—the borrowed glow!

Herein is found the exciting credential of the Christian faith—the borrowed glow, the likeness of Jesus reflected in the life of the believer. This magnificent reflection and likeness of our Lord is no "happen so" nor accident in time. It is heaven's knighthood upon the chosen vessel who will take time for the eternal, look for the burning bush and pray for the borrowed glow.

> O Lord, since I have no luster worth the look,
> Nor beauty of my own to show;
> Make me a mirror for Thy Son
> Reflecting but a borrowed glow.

2

An Attitude for Attainment

For as he thinketh in his heart, so is he. Proverbs 23:7

Some time ago my responsibility led me to Minden, Louisiana. While there I lunched with a pastor friend. During the meal a member of his congregation came by our table and without meaning to be humorous at all she said, "Pastor, another day like tomorrow and we've had it!" In that sentence is reflected an attitude and disposition that is not only defeative but also dangerous. To feel that tomorrow is lost, that there is no possibility of a good day, to see oneself as a part of a failing cause or a traveler on a sinking ship, to look upon the future as hopeless and upon mankind as utterly helpless beyond reparation is to possess all the ingredients necessary for failure as a person, student, family member, or world citizen. This attitude which is so commonplace these days has within itself the virus of destruction and the power to rob life of its zest and reason. It is the germ that breeds stagnation, the stigma that strangles attainment. We concern ourselves with this attitude for I am firmly persuaded it is absolutely relevant and vital to the issues and answers of our time.

From God's inspired Word comes the statement: "For as he thinketh in his heart, so is he" (Prov. 23:7). What a provocative statement! To believe it is to know that man is more than blood, bone, and brawn. He is more than cell and sinew, more than food and drink. Man cannot live by bread alone. He is what he thinks. He is what he values most, loves most, and dreams most. Man is the sum total of his allegiances.

What is your attitude toward life? The answer given will be equated by the things you hold to be precious. That will form your attitude. The attitude you bring to life will make it a heaven or a hell on earth.

There Is Much to Discourage

It does not take an ancient seer or even a modern mystic to know that in the beloved Robert Browning's beautiful *Pippa Passes*, Pippa is carried beyond reality when she sings, "God's in his heaven—All's right with the world." It is certainly true that God is in his heaven, but all is not right with the world. It is a frightening world! As we look out on our world, it often appears to have gone stark mad. It is full of grim and harrowing things. Often we feel so helpless as we watch the human situation deteriorating. Fury and violence and a mounting hate become our nation's daily diary. Our never-reeling, uptight citizenry watch like spectators at a shoot out. The wonder is not that we should sometimes be afraid, but that we should ever be free from fear if we look only at visible facts. Where is there one of us who is not disturbed by the lawbreakers and the murderers, the rapist and the drug merchant, the plight of our schools and universities, the miseries of war?

War

George Wall of Harvard tells us that "Russia and the U.S. alone have stockpiled nuclear weapons with the explosive power of fifteen tons of TNT for every man, woman, and child on earth. A few ounces adequately distributed would be enough to kill each person, but we have produced an overkill of thirty thousand pounds for every human being on earth."

Senator Mark Hatfield at a recent conference said, "Many postulate that the 'balance of terror' is the only trustworthy condition of peace. Since World War II we have spent over one trillion dollars for military purposes—for weapons, soldiers, and the machinery of war—to insure the proper balance."

Pollution

Because of undisciplined technology, vast quantities of waste, pollutants, and contaminants are poisoning our environment. Dr. James A. Oliver, Coordinator of Scientific and Environmental Programs of the American Museum of Natural History, reminds that "in the U.S. alone we annually dump 350 billion tons of garbage and sewage, 1 billion tons of mining waste, 48 billion metal cans, 20 million tons of paper, and 7 million worn out automobiles; and we pour 142 million tons of smoke and noxious fumes into the air we breathe." At a recent convention Dr. William M. Pinson, former Professor of Christian Ethics at Southwestern Baptist Theological Seminary and presently pastor of the First Baptist Church of Wichita Falls, Texas, said, "If the human breed does not burn himself to death, or war himself to death, he may succeed in choking himself to death on his own pollution."

We are confronted with the consequences of our scientific skills: the fall of a sparrow does signal our destiny. The race problem is not something "out there" that can be fixed by hiring an expert to do it. Détente does not guarantee the alleviation of atomic annihilation. All matters are interrelated. For today and tomorrow every solution is personal and must be dealt with in the depths of every human heart. Oh yes, the situation is frightening!

An Attitude for Attainment

Population Explosion

And then there is the problem of our ever-exploding population. Wallace Hamilton called it *The Thunder of Bare Feet*. During the next minute 234 babies will be born. By this time tomorrow the net population of the world will have been increased by a mass of 190,000 individuals.

Eugene Gottmon is responsible for the term *megalopolis* which speaks of the crowded earth littered by the living. We think of megalopolis in terms of Tokyo, Hong Kong, London and yet fail to realize that the most populated spot on earth lies between Alexandria, Virginia, and Boston, Massachusetts. It is one sprawling nonstop city including Washington, Trenton, New York and Boston. One-fifth of all the people in the U.S. are living on one-fiftieth of the land surface in the Northeast. It has been projected that by the year 2000, the New York, Boston, and Washington area with its solid city will extend to Minneapolis, Minnesota. Denver and St. Louis will have grown together. New Orleans, Houston, San Antonio, and Dallas will become one great continuing city. Unattached multitudes will be "holed up" in high rise apartments. By 1985, it is estimated that the average American will spend 60% of his entire lifetime in an apartment complex. Forty percent of all housing in the U.S. is now apartments. John Chancellor said recently: "We will have to build a city the size of Atlanta, Georgia, every eighty days to keep up with the population increase."

Technological Advances

To these already mentioned problems add the challenge of technological advances which suggest that this decade will experience the perfection of the control of man's mind. Experience to any depths will be available on order using chemical, psychological and physical stimulants. Imagine possessing the power to control man's body and mind!

Consider also the problem of regimented materialism—the "tyranny of things." *Newsweek* magazine has described our day as a "time of ultimate miracle products giving indulgence without penalties, experience without risk, deprivation without deprival. Gluttony can now be non-fattening, lust can be non-procreative, and even thought can be reduced to a complex of magnetic tapes, transistors, and computer cards."

Humanism

Today's world insists that one face the frontier of scientific humanism and intellectual snobbery. Blend with these characteristics the world's lack of concern for the great masses of unwanted and unwashed. Take note that more than half of the people of the earth have never gone to bed once in their lives with a full stomach; ten thousand people die every week because they just do not have anything to eat. Does the big picture begin to come into focus? Ours is an aching, throbbing, frightening, challenging world, and it needs what you are and what you can do! I am desperately concerned that there be revolution in our hearts, or else there will be revolution in our streets. God help us never to lose the capacity to care, to feel deeply and everlastingly about the hurt in our brother's heart!

Spiritual Menace

An injustice would be done if I failed to emphasize what I consider the most dangerous menace of all: the loss of faith—the forsaking of one's confidence in God.

Have you sensed it? Do you feel its loss in our cities and neighborhoods? Have you observed the secularization of our society? As I see it, this is the saddest sight on the national horizon—a nation in danger of forsaking its faith! A man can survive anything but that. He can face it all, however wounding—death, scandal, separation, business reversals, illness, loneliness, all of it—so long as his faith is firmly resting in God Almighty. But when his faith begins to fail, there is life's greatest peril.

And is this not our greatest enemy? It is not so much the plunderers of our properties but the plunderers of our souls, the marauders of our minds, the vandals of our faith—faith in ourselves, in our nation and above all faith in God, our absolute necessity.

The Dignity of Choice

You have the God-endowed right to choose what course you will take and what attitude you will bring to bear upon your generation. God has created human life with the dignity of will—the individual gift of personal decision. No one is a robot controlled by buttons and switches, bending and bowing as a plaything of fate. Rather, you are men and women dignified with the freedom and right of God-given choice. That choice must be made! You and you alone decide whether to retire from the field of life's battles: to forfeit the fight for moral integrity and human worth, to steal away and live in midget-like mediocrity. Yes, you must choose!

Society has spawned a whole school of men who are determined to see how little they can do and how much they can get. Rudyard Kipling pays his respects to those looters, loafers, and loungers in his poem "Mary's Son."

> If you stop to find out what your wages will be
>   And how they will clothe and feed you,
> Willie, my son, don't you go on the sea,
>   For the Sea will never need you.
>
> If you ask for the reason of every command,
>   And argue with people about you,

Willie, my son, don't you go on the Land,
  For the Land will do better without you.

If you stop to consider the work you have done
  And to boast what your labour is worth, dear,
Angels may come for you, Willie, my son,
  But you'll never be wanted on Earth, dear!

You may choose to join the quitters and complainers, the placard bearers and protesters, the "something for nothing" addicts. You may decide to cast your lot with that delegation dedicated to defaming our blessed heritage, or it is your privilege to accept the challenge of this good earth with its good and its bad, its cross and its crown. Should your decision be the latter, and I pray to God it is, be assured you have chosen no easy mark.

It has always been costly to be a builder or a roadmaker. Trailblazers and truth-seekers pay a heavy toll for the right of way of change. Cross-bearers are hard to come by these days, but after all, isn't that what life is all about?

It takes more of a man to stand tall in the land,
  Than it has ever taken before;
It costs more for the few to be loyal and true,
  It costs more to be one who restores.

But there'll always be those who believe in their souls,
  That to compromise would be sin;
And that's reason enough to have faith and look up,
  Heaven bless them—God's leaders of men!

A Better World

There can be a better world. I believe that with all my heart! For regardless of the circumstance the world is in, history remains under God's sovereignty. In Ephesians, Paul

An Attitude for Attainment

writes that God "purposes in his sovereign will . . . that everything that exists in Heaven or earth shall find its perfection and fulfillment in him" (Eph. 1:9–10, Phillips).

This is no idle dream. It is secured upon the proposition with which we started. Truth will triumph. It must, for it is validated in the moral nature of God. As long as we believe in the value of a single life, the worth of a human soul, as long as we believe in the power for good inherent in the life of one dedicated man or woman, there is hope! As long as we believe in having a hand in world good instead of having a hand out for the world's goods and truly believe that giving is more important than getting, there is still hope for the world in which we live.

En route to negotiate a cease-fire between Katanga and the United Nations forces, Dag Hammarskjöld died in a fiery plane crash in Northern Rhodesia. The scholarly, mystical Christian had been the United Nations' Secretary General for eight years. Only two months before his death he had written in his diary entitled *Markings*:

> Tired
> And lonely,
> So tired
> The heart aches.
> Meltwater trickles
> Down the rocks,
> The fingers are numb,
> The knees tremble.
> It is now,
> Now that you must not give in.
> On the path of the others
> Are resting places,
> Places in the sun
> Where they can meet.

> But this
> Is your path,
> And it is now,
> Now, that you must not fail.
>
> Weep
> If you can,
> Weep,
> But do not complain.
> The way chose you—
> And you must be thankful.

I love those last two lines: "The way chose you—And you must be thankful."

You stand upon the scene of today's happenings because God chose you for it. You did not choose it nor plan the moment of your own existence. God did. It is this knowledge and assurance that enables you to look up and believe that there can and will be a better world.

All of us need to be reminded that we do not walk alone. The bearer of the strong name of the Trinity is with us. He has given his word: "Lo, I am with you alway, even unto the end of the world" (Matt. 28:20). We need nothing more. It is enough. With this promise to rest upon, I for one can say:

> Is it wrong to dream
> of a world made clean,
> Of its greed of its vile extreme?
> Is it wrong to plan for a whole new land,
> Where a man is free, really free?
>
> Will there come a day,
> such a bright new day,
> Every fear will be laid aside?

An Attitude for Attainment

When the children's sound from the streets abound,
And the young find hope once again?

Could it happen here,
'mid these warsome years,
As we pray anxious prayers for peace;
That a spiritual thirst
Might so fill the earth,
All mankind would kneel at His feet?

Chorus:
I will have my dream,
Come and dream with me,
We can change the world,
if our hearts believe.
'Tho some would laugh and scorn,
make a mockery—
I believe in God,
I will have my dream.
—"I Will Have My Dream"

3

Made for the Mountains

He maketh my feet like hinds' feet, and setteth me upon my high places. Psalm 18:33

God made the whole earth beautiful, but nothing is more beautiful than the mountains. Their majesty and splendor, snow-capped ranges, the glory of their towering grace speak in a language all its own. Little wonder then that the setting of this shepherd's psalm is in the mountains.

The land of Palestine was burned brown for much of the year. It was the custom of the nomadic shepherd to lead his sheep into the hill country. Only in the uplands could he find green grass and refreshing streams.

It was in just such a setting that the Psalmist-Shepherd of Israel, gazing off toward the beauty of the mountainous terrain saw a sight so arresting and stimulating he could not turn his eyes away. High on one of the mountain trails was a red fallow deer. The deer was native to this part of the country and physically equipped to scale the heights. The longer the shepherd watched the more intrigued he became. The deer blended perfectly into that mountainside and was pressing toward the summit. Nothing could detain it. Obviously it was made for the mountains.

The mind of the Psalmist was completely captivated by this sight so full of spiritual implication. And he burst into singing, "He maketh my feet like hinds' feet, and setteth me upon my high places." The shepherd saw the red deer as emblematic and representative of the God-follower.

Made for the Mountains

Every genuine follower of Christ has his mountain to climb. A world of adventure awaits those who will dare to do the will of God and seek out his place on the Master's Matterhorn.

To watch the red deer with the shepherd is to marvel at its egality and sure-footedness. Seldom does it step backwards or find the path untenable. A quiet steadiness is obvious. Within the animal is a God-given nature that draws and beckons it upward, always higher.

Christians are like that. They are made for the mountains. God has equipped his crowning creation with the capacity to enter into fellowship with him. He has given man the unique ability to love, to have faith, to feel compassion, to express concern and to communicate these feelings as a child of God. Someone has very beautifully reminded that the heart of man is a God-shaped blank and can only be satisfied through fellowship with him. It is expressed so effectively in the Book of Job as the writer explains, "Thine hands have made me and fashioned me together round about; . . . Thou hast clothed me with skin and flesh, and hast fenced me with bones and sinews. Thou hast granted me life and favour, and thy visitation hath preserved my spirit" (Job 10:8, 11, 12). Man is made for fellowship with God—made for the mountains!

To see the red deer in the mountain setting is to be impressed not only by the physical make-up of the animal but also with the nature within the animal that draws it to the elevated plateaus and the highland trails. It would be out of character to see this particular animal loitering in the lowlands. God has made it for the high places, and it would be unsafe anywhere else.

With the miracle of regeneration comes the divine impartation of a new nature. This new nature is the nature of Christ (Rom. 7:14-25). Old things lose their luster and value. All things become new, meaningful, fresh and exciting. God's miracle of new birth has occurred and nothing will ever be the same again. Within the human heart is implanted a new nature. The Holy Spirit comes to indwell in the body of the believer, and this new kind of man looks up toward the mountains with a longing to know and do the will of God.

This longing is so strikingly expressed by Paul in Romans 8:11, "But if the Spirit of him that raised up Jesus from the dead dwell in you, he that raised up Christ from the dead shall also quicken your mortal bodies by his Spirit that dwelleth in you." To know Christ is to know a sense of divine stirring that leads toward the upward stairs of high and holy and mountainous living. Those who are truly born of God are never, never again satisfied with the stagnant swamps and dark marshes of sinful living. The real Christian can never be comfortable in a sin-filled atmosphere. He will not settle for Satan's second best nor be satisfied with an imitation of the real thing for his eyes have seen the King and now there is room for no other.

Tried By the Trail

It is never easy to climb a mountain. It was not easy for the red deer. It is not easy for the Christian venturer. Patience and endurance are absolute necessities for those who have eyes for the spiritual skyline. Trails that Christians must take are often treacherous ones. Nowhere in the Word is the follower of Christ promised an easy journey. However, the Christian trailblazer is given an assurance and confidence which comes from being tried by the trail. The conflicts and crises that are a part of the climb are to be understood and interpreted as a part of God's program of discipleship. This is true of every boulder of difficulty, every landslide of disappointment, and every onslaught of the evil one. God has promised an empowering, a special enduement, a special spiritual stamina sufficient for every extremity one may face on life's pathway.

He equips his child with whatever shoes the journey requires. In a picturesque metaphor we read, "Thy shoes shall be iron and brass" (Deut. 33:25). How encouraging to know that our feet will be shod for the road wherever that road may lead.

Some time ago there was an interesting article concerning mountain climbers and mountain peaks. A portion of the article read: "The government of Nepal charges admission prices to climb the mountain. For instance you must buy a ticket costing $630 before being permitted to attempt the 29,028 ft. Mount Everest. Cut-rate tickets are offered for lower peaks."

It was that last sentence that made headlines in my heart: "Cut-rate tickets are offered for lower peaks." I suppose anyone could settle for less than God's best. Millions do it daily. Multitudes have undertaken the trek toward the summit of God's finest and best only to settle for the mediocrity of lower peaks. What a tragedy! What a waste! The lyrics of John Oatman's well-known hymn "Higher Ground" are filled with challenge at this point.

> My heart has no desire to stay
> Where doubts arise and fears dismay;
> Tho' some may dwell where these abound,
> My prayer, my aim is higher ground.
>
> Lord, lift me up and let me stand,

> By faith, on heaven's tableland,
> A higher plane than I have found;
> Lord, plant my feet on higher ground.

One of the most encouraging facets of spiritual trailblazing and mountain climbing is the discovery that one has been there before. Jesus Christ, the file leader of our faith, never calls upon us to journey into any experience nor pursue any path without proceeding ahead of us to mark the trail and show the way (John 14:5, 6). Encouragement, warm and personal, comes from the Word with the reminder that Christ "is able to keep you from falling, and to present you faultless before the presence of his glory with exceeding joy" (Jude 24).

Some years ago I read a story by Harold Dye, a gifted Christian writer. Mr. Dye said that while on a fishing trip in the New Mexico mountains he was impressed to try his luck in a stream much higher up the mountain trail. He had the proverbial "fisherman's feeling" that this very special stream was brimful of mountain trout. Mr. Dye said, "I could hardly wait to get to that stream. However, as I rounded a corner along the infrequently traveled trail, I discovered the winter rains and snow thaws had left a chasm in the trail. To get to the other side would necessitate quite a leap—a dangerous leap at that." He continued, "As I debated making the leap from this side to the other I noticed something on the trail ahead that made all the difference in the world—the fresh imprint of a shoe. Someone had been along this trail before me. He too had faced the same chasm and had safely crossed it. That was all the encouragement I needed. With one strong effort I was safely on the other side and on my way to that inviting stream." That story illustrates so realistically the Bible's promise that God will mark the trail and show the way for his trusting child.

Made for the Mountains

God has a place for every planned creation
A path for every star to go.
He drew the course for every river's journey,
Now I know He has a way for me.
—"His Way—Mine!"

Safest in the Mountains

Consider once again the red fallow deer spoken of by the Psalmist. Another spiritual truth is impressively illustrated. The deer is safest in the mountains. It is interesting to note that even as David was writing this Psalm he was being stalked and endangered by the malice of Saul. He had found shelter in the crags of the rocks and safety in the high mountain pass. Thus he sang, "He maketh my feet like hinds' feet, and setteth me upon my high places."

It is no less true that the child of God is safest and most secure when standing high upon the mountain of God's perfect will. As it would be perilous for the hind to live in the lowlands, it is equally perilous for a Christian to dwell there. Satan prowls the earth like a lurking lion seeking whom he may destroy (1 Pet. 5:8). Is it any wonder then that the safest place for the believer is high upon Sonrise Mountain? The Christian yielded and surrendered to the will of God is safer on some narrow dangerous ledge of life looking into the very face of death than he would be on some flat fruited plain outside the will of God.

During the Chinese-Japanese War an American missionary doctor was performing an operation. In the midst of the operation there was an air raid, and bombs began bursting in the nearby courtyard. A Christian nurse insisted that the doctor seek shelter lest he be destroyed by the bomb. To this plea the missionary doctor replied, "Young lady, the safest place on earth is in the center of the will of God."

There is no doubt that the safest place on earth for the Christian is in the center of the will of God.

Represents the Mountains

A last look at the red fallow deer brings the reminder that it represents the mountains. To gaze upon one of these mountain animals is to be reminded automatically of their native habitat. It is natural to respond that way.

To look upon the great American eagle with its wings spread, talons taut, and eyes full of wildfire is to paint on the canvas of the mind a picture of the high country. The eagle is made for the mountains. Nothing less than that setting would be becoming. Nothing less would be representative.

Some years ago while pastoring in the city of Fort Worth, Texas, I took my two sons to the zoo to see the animals. We saw them all—the lions, the tigers, the bears. And like everyone else we eventually gravitated to the monkeys' cage to watch their antics. It was then that my second son, often more adventuresome and outspoken, shouted loudly enough to stampede the whole menagerie of jungle beasts and said, "Dad, that one looks just like Mrs. _____." He called the name of one of our deacons' wives. I almost died! Following my first impulse, I glanced swiftly to the right and to the left to be sure she was not in the vicinity. Then, using the third parental voice, which I might add is the voice of authority, I said, "Son, that was such an unkind thing to say, and I am disappointed in you. What would Mrs. _____ think if she heard you say such a thing? Now run along and see the other animals, but don't ever talk like that again!" As he ran ahead I looked back at that animal he had described and must admit it did look a lot like that deacon's wife!

All of us have at one time or another looked at some

Made for the Mountains

little new baby and have been impressed by the strong family resemblance. It always pleases a mother or father to have someone say the child is the very image of the parent. This is as it should be. The child is a representative of the family. If this is true in the physical relationships of life it is even more true in the spiritual. The Christian is a member of God's family by virtue of birth—the new birth. As a child of God he is to be a living reminder in conduct and character of the Saviour Jesus Christ.

In His Steps

Made for the mountains! That is the challenge Christ has given to his followers. Nothing more, nothing less. "For even hereunto were ye called: because Christ also suffered for us, leaving us an example, that ye should follow his steps" (1 Pet. 2:21). To follow Christ is to walk in the steps of a mountain man. He came from the heights of heaven, preached his greatest sermon on the mountain, was transfigured on Mount Hermon, prayed on Mount Olivet, died on Mount Calvary, descended from the Mount of Olives. Jesus was a man mountainous in his compassion, in his love, in his plan and program of redemption and in his promises. He was a mountain man. No one can follow him and desire less than the mountain life. His kind of spiritual kinsmen are made for the mountains.

There is a beautiful story that occurred in Switzerland. A beloved mountain guide slipped on a high incline and fell to his death. The villagers wanted to commemorate the life of the great guide and commissioned a sculptor to carve his likeness and place it at the exact location where he fell. The sculptor complied and characteristically presented the guide in his Alpine hat, cleated shoes, rope and pickaxe in hand. It was shaped showing the guide in the very act of climbing the mountain. To epitomize their friend's life these words were placed at the base of the statue: "He died climbing."

We cannot know when God may choose to lift us from our mountain of responsibility into the fullness of life everlasting. But of this one thing we can be sure: We have been made for the mountains and whenever he calls we should be found climbing. "He maketh my feet like hinds' feet, and setteth me upon my high places." Made for the mountains!

4

A Disposable Religion

> But a certain man named Ananias, with Sapphira his wife, sold a possession,
> And kept back part of the price, his wife also being privy to it, and brought a certain part, and laid it at the apostles' feet.
> But Peter said, Ananias, why hath Satan filled thine heart to lie to the Holy Ghost, and to keep back part of the price of the land?
> Whiles it remained, was it not thine own? and after it was sold, was it not in thine own power? why hast thou conceived this thing in thine heart? thou hast not lied unto men, but unto God. Acts 5:1–4

Some time ago I visited a Christian bookstore convention. One exhibit was unusually fascinating. As a part of their wares, there was displayed a disposable communion cup. It was advertised as being so inexpensive you could "just throw it away." I suppose this godly gadgetry represented just another convenience for our fast moving society of sophisticates. There are so many conveniences and changes that we are experiencing these days. We are all aware of the constant scientific development and inventive genius which is so much a part of the lifestyle of our time.

Rocket fuels have already been developed to carry man coast to coast in ten minutes and around the world in a day. Within another decade or two it could be possible for one to eat breakfast in the United States, enjoy lunch in Australia and return home in time for dinner.

I read recently that five million children in remote areas will learn their reading, writing and arithmetic from television sets receiving signals from the American satellite 22,300 miles above the Indian Ocean. For thousands of these children it will be their first classroom experience and also their first exposure to television.

We are instructed that in the future every person will have a portable phone and can dial anywhere in the world. The secretary can type a letter at her desk and then, in a fraction of a second, send it to its destination by satellite "Telemail."

Hospitals will have diagnostic treatment centers tied into medical facilities and computers all over the world.

Housewives will be able to do their shopping without ever leaving home by picture phones that scan the shelves of local grocery stores. You can order, the store clerk will pull the card, fill the order and deliver it to your home. The bill will be sent later. What conveniences!

This is also the "throw away" age with its throw-away toothbrushes, throw-away ball point pens, throw-away paper clothing and throw-away morals.

In this mobile, moving, restless nation of ours we are now introduced to throw-away communion cups—an innovative new kind of convenience for church folks. One cannot help wondering what will be offered next in the area of holy hardware. It should not be too surprising to hear of one-a-day plastic prayer pills, comfort by cassette, bottled baptism, certificates of character, credit card compassion, and scars by mail.

Compromise and Convenience

This tendency toward a religion of compromise is wide-

A Disposable Religion

spread. Many are uncomfortable with the faith of our fathers and the lifestyle of our Lord. There is a considerable number who feel the need of a religion of convenience—really, a disposable religion, a faith and fare that can be used when needed and disposed of when it becomes confining or demanding.

Such a religion could be used when trouble comes, disaster strikes or crisis appears. It could be entirely disposable should it interrupt one's leisure or recreation. Disposable if it distracts from a party that is being planned or if it convicts of the conduct being performed. Disposable if it annoys friends or associates. Disposable if it arrests in any way a certain amourising. Disposable if it castigates one's compromising. Disposable if it stands in disagreement with the community interest or standards. Disposable if it calls for changing the habits in the home or throws a damper on the office party. Disposable if it forbids drunkenness and worldly habits. Disposable if it does not allow sexual promiscuity. Disposable if it is too strict on the children. A disposable religion.

Ananias and Sapphira

A striking illustration of this religion of convenience appears in Acts 5 in the Bible episode of Ananias and Sapphira. These two church-going saints determined that the sale of a piece of property was a bit too advantageous to share. They determined to lie about the price they received, and although they made an offering it was hypocritical and disrespectful of the atmosphere in which they lived. Both dropped dead while the church family looked on. This marked the first instant funeral.

Their religion was of the disposable variety. No doubt they were voting members of the church. In fact, their background and testimony indicates that they had been used of the Lord. Certainly they had chosen to walk a rather unpopular walk and had stood with the company of the committed in a time when it was dangerous to do so. Many good things could be said about this couple. It had not been demanded that they sell their property nor that they contribute to the love offering. The sin in their life was that they disposed of their convictions and pursued a religion of convenience and compromise. They tried by pretention to appear to be what they were not. It is a sobering and penetrating revelation that the presence of the Holy Spirit and such hypocritical conduct could not coexist in the same room.

Can you imagine the consternation that would occur should our churches today be so genuinely Christlike, so led of the Holy Spirit, that it would be literally dangerous for anyone to make a profession or a commitment that was false and hypocritical! The fact is, it is dangerous to play the hypocrite.

Biblical Examples

Throughout the pages of the Bible such conduct is illustrated. Always there is the strongest denunciation and rebuke for those who practice a disposable religion.

Saul wanted God to give him victory over the Amalekites. But after the victory he insisted on negotiating the peace alone (1 Sam. 15).

David wanted religion enough to help him defeat Goliath but not one that would deny him the beautiful lady Bathsheba who was bathing on the balcony (1 Sam. 11).

Jonah wanted a revival everywhere with the exception of Ninevah. The Ninevites were the wrong color (Jon. 1:3).

Herod enjoyed hearing John the Baptist preach until John pointed out the Herodias in his life. He then felt

A Disposable Religion

impelled to dispose of this religion of specifics by cutting off the Baptist's head (Mark 6).

The rich young ruler was ready to follow Jesus until he realized this followship would affect his pocketbook (Mark 10:17-22).

The villagers of Nazareth were excited about hearing their young townsman speak until he announced that he was the Messiah. They then determined that he was the wrong Jesus and offered him exit off the edge of a cliff (Luke 4:16-32).

The herdsmen of Gadara were perfectly happy for the wild man in the tombs to be healed of his insanity until it cost them their pigs. Then it became perfectly obvious that the pigs were more important to them than the person (Mark 5).

These Bible vignettes have their counterpart on today's scene. It is not difficult to detect the chameleon-like Christian who talks much further than he walks. What could be more damaging to the cause of the Carpenter of Nazareth than a man or woman whose religion is disposable?

In view of this unholy hypocrisy it is little wonder that there are multitudes of folk who cannot be convinced that the Christianity confessed by the pious pretender is the same as that personified in the Christ of the Cross.

A Startling Suggestion

May I offer a suggestion that could have a life-changing effect upon those who give it serious thought? Suppose for a moment that the salvation made possible and available to us by the coming of Jesus Christ was a disposable salvation. What would be your disposition should the New Testament be declared invalid, discontinued until further notice? Suppose God changed his mind about saving us from the horrible bondage, slavery and penalty of sin.

Imagine, if you can, the desperate plight of all mankind should the vicarious suffering of Christ be discredited and counted null and void? No greater tragedy could befall mankind than the tragedy of a disposable salvation!

Dependable Grace

Thank God this matter is not on trial! The glory and magnificence of God's saving grace is rooted in dependability and steadfastness.

"Know therefore that the Lord thy God, he is God, the faithful God, which keepeth covenant and mercy with them that love him and keep his commandments to a thousand generations" (Deut. 7:9).

"God is faithful, by whom ye were called unto the fellowship of his Son Jesus Christ our Lord" (1 Cor. 1:9).

"That by two immutable things, in which it was impossible for God to lie, we might have a strong consolation, who have fled for refuge to lay hold upon the hope set before us: Which hope we have as an anchor of the soul, both sure and stedfast" (Heb. 6:18–19a).

God's word is unchangeable as he is unchangeable. "Heaven and earth shall pass away: but my words shall not pass away" (Mark 13:31). His promises are sure and secure. "Let us hold fast the profession of our faith without wavering; (for he is faithful that promised;)" (Heb. 10:23).

The very nature of God validates the trustworthiness of his grace. Without this assurance life would be a catastrophe and death a sad finality. But with this blessed assurance comes life at its unending best and joy superlative!

"I am come that they might have life, and that they might have it more abundantly" (John 10:10).

In light of what the believer has in and through Christ, it would be utterly unthinkable and completely irrational for one to entertain the slightest thought of disposing of God's unspeakable gift.

Rather let all the redeemed join in chorus to praise our Eternal King for a salvation as real as God, as sure as the Son, and as true as the open tomb.

5

Come Rest Awhile

> And the apostles gathered themselves together unto Jesus, and told him all things, both what they had done, and what they had taught.
> And he said unto them, Come ye yourselves apart into a desert place, and rest a while. Mark 6:30–31

Here is a Bible presentation so alive with human needs, so absolutely personal to Christian health, so immensely practical in its exhortation, one dare not miss it. It is a message for everyone that has ever felt disillusioned or disappointed. It offers help for all of those that have known the cutting edge of frustration, the bitter dregs of disheartenment. Beyond question this spiritual truth is an absolute necessity for the maintenance of Christian health and happiness.

The disciples of Jesus had returned from a journey both spiritually satisfying and physically exhausting. Theirs had been a commission to share the message of Christ in new fields of opportunity. They had done their work well and had conducted themselves in a manner becoming to true servants of Christ. It had been an exciting and victorious adventure. But in the midst of it all these followers of Christ had become worn in body and spirit. The strain of spiritual battle had taken its toll. And, as if this were not enough, they were sick at heart because of the murder of John the Baptist. He had represented a sentinel of moral integrity and steel-like courage. Add an anxiousness about the future and you have a portrait of despair.

No doubt the disciples wondered what Jesus would say to them upon their return. Would it be a word of sternness for not having had more success? Would he insist that they accept additional assignments and immediately proceed to a new undertaking? Would there be a word of commendation for their efforts? Thus they arrived in the presence of the Master.

Jesus, the wise Jesus, knowing their condition far better than they themselves knew it, said, "Come ye yourselves apart into a desert place, and rest a while" (Mark 6:31). In the hours that followed they were to rest physically by a boat trip on the Sea of Galilee, mentally while they listened to Jesus speak, and spiritually as they witnessed another of his miraculous works.

With the admonishment to "rest awhile," our Lord gave to his disciples for all times a prescription for maintaining spiritual health. It has never changed and is as expedient for today's disciples as yesterday's apostles. It is obvious that he gave to them the plan he himself followed. To observe the life of Christ is to see him turning aside from the press of the crowds and crises to "rest awhile" in communion and fellowship with the Father.

"And in the morning, rising up a great while before day, he went out, and departed into a solitary place, and there prayed" (Mark 1:35).

"And when he had sent them away, he departed into a mountain to pray" (Mark 6:46).

"But so much the more went there a fame abroad of him: and great multitudes came together to hear, and to be healed by him of their infirmities. And he withdrew himself into the wilderness, and prayed" (Luke 5:15–16).

"And it came to pass in those days, that he went out into

a mountain to pray, and continued all night in prayer to God" (Luke 6:12).

"And he was withdrawn from them about a stone's cast, and kneeled down, and prayed, Saying, Father . . . not my will, but thine, be done" (Luke 22:41–42).

Jesus felt it was necessary and important to draw aside for spiritual restoration and refreshment. If this was a necessity for our Lord, it is especially necessary for all of us who love him and want to be like him. How desperately we need to follow his example and draw aside to the secret place of his presence and there find the rest promised every child of God (Matt. 11:28).

Our Swift and Changing World

Ours is a swift-moving, changing world. Each day reminds us that things are not as they were. It is difficult to keep pace no matter what "drummer" we hear! These changing times are epitomized in the poem "Remember When?" written by Othell Hand:

Remember when hippie meant big in the hips,
And a trip involved cars, planes, and ships.
And pot was a vessel for cooking things in,
And hooked was what Grandmother's rug might have been.
When neat meant well organized, tidy and clean,
And grass was a ground cover, normally green.
When lights, and not people, were turned on and off,
And the pill could be what you took for a cough.
When fuzz was a substance fluffy like lint,
And bread came from bakeries, not from the mint.
When square meant a 90 degree angle form,
And cool was a temperature, not quite warm.
When roll was a bun, and rock was a stone,
And hangup was what you could do with a phone.

Come Rest Awhile 51

When chicken meant poultry and bag meant a sack,
And junk, trashy cast offs and old brick-a-brack.
When swinger was someone who swung in a swing,
And pad was a soft sort of cushiony thing.
When dig meant to shovel and spade in the dirt,
And put on is what you would do with a shirt.
Words once so sensible, sober, and serious
Are making the freak scene like psycho delirious.
It's groovy, man, groovy but English it's not
Me thinks that the language has gone straight to pot.

Yes, ours is a changing world and the problems are mountainous. Scores of professing Christians identify with the sentiments expressed in the theatrical production of a few years ago, *Stop the World, I Want To Get Off*.

The Exhaustive Pace of Life

Someone prayed a rather descriptive prayer recently in the words, "Dear Lord and Father of Mankind, forgive our feverish ways." Most of us feel we are constantly under pressure. The schedules we keep, the demands and responsibilities that are ours, plus the absorption of the trivial are enough to drive one up the proverbial wall! Amidst the noise and strain of our workaday world it is more the usual than the unusual to see someone coming apart mentally, socially, and spiritually.

Where is there a one of us who has not at times felt wrung out, exhausted, and totally useless to the work we are called upon to perform?

The Fight To Do Right

The journey to which Christ calls was never meant to be an easy one. It is a daily struggle and confrontation with "the prince of the power of the air" (Eph. 2:2).

"For we wrestle not against flesh and blood, but against principalities, against powers, against the rulers of the darkness of this world, against spiritual wickedness in high places" (Eph. 6:12).

"Your adversary the devil, as a roaring lion, walketh about, seeking whom he may devour" (1 Pet. 5:8).

It would be the height of audacity to minimize the power and cunning of the great antagonist, the Devil. Every Christian must recognize the adversary for what he is and be prepared for his evil maneuvers.

Spiritual Exhaustion

Strange as it may seem, there is a drain upon one's spiritual strength while engaged in unselfish service and witnessing.

As Jesus was on his way to heal the daughter of Jairus, a woman desperately anxious to be healed from her own tragic illness, touched the hem of his garment and was instantly made whole. How provocative and meaningful is the sentence that follows:

"And Jesus, immediately knowing in himself that virtue had gone out of him, turned him about in the press, and said, Who touched my clothes?" (Mark 5:30).

Her healing had not come about without the absorption of strength from our Lord. With every work done in Jesus' name there is a depletion of strength commensurate with the service wrought. This in itself should be enough to cause the child of God to take time for spiritual rest and recuperation.

One cannot live razor-sharp and heaven-high every moment! The level of fever pitch is dangerous. As fire and steam must be kept under control, so the Christian's temperament and testimony must be under the Master's control. I am suspicious of the glassy-eyed religious activist who never seems to need a time apart with God.

Will we never learn that one can become exhausted

spiritually as well as physically? That a spiritual breakdown can be experienced just as surely as can a physical one? It is tragic to see someone suffer such a breakdown and never get over it. What a loss to the cause of Christ!

The Necessity of Spiritual Rest

Like a spring that is wound too tight, machinery overworked, soldiers too long at the front, pilots too long at the controls, a child of God may become overworked and need a period of quiet restoration and soul recharging.

Amid the sound of squealing tires, jet planes, transistor radios and the constant badgering of the advertising media, every Christian needs to experience the therapy of withdrawal. There is a curative power and a healing quality in spiritual rest.

The successful Christian life is not equated by polished rhetorics, personal talents, organizational abilities nor even gifted creativity. Rather, one's spiritual value is determined by how well one learns to lean upon the Lord and draw upon his strength. A beautiful paraphrase of Philippians 4:13 is rendered, "I can do all things through Christ who keeps on pouring power into me."

The influence we exert upon the world around us is only as potent and strong as the quality of our personal life. That quality is only possible when time is taken for the great things of the soul. Edna St. Vincent Millay wrote in her poem "Renascence":

> The world stands out on either side
> No wider than the heart is wide;
> Above the world is stretched the sky,—
> No higher than the soul is high.

In the Strength of the Flesh

The disciples who returned to the side of Christ were

weary from their mission, but they could have gone on to further tasks had the Lord commanded. However, it is likely their work would have been carried on in the strength of the flesh and not in the power of the Spirit. How great is the danger of growing weary in well doing! All of us have known individuals who have lost their enthusiasm and boldness. We have known those whose spiritual nerve has been severed resulting in the loss of a sensitivity to sacred things.

Others have become critical and ill-tempered because of the neglect of a time apart with God. Instead of an attitude of concerned love and compassion there is demonstrated an attitude of offense that would "call fire from heaven" and destroy the opposition.

A final result of a life lived "in the strength of the flesh" is spiritual unemployment. Those who depend upon themselves and find no need for a time alone with God soon become dropouts and quitters.

Come Rest Awhile

Few seem able to hear the "still, small voice of God." Do you suppose it is because of the loss of a listening ear? Some musicians pride themselves on having perfect pitch. Skilled mechanics can listen to the sound of a motor and detect whether or not a problem is present. Foresters know the meaning of every sound in the forest. Is it any less important for the child of God to be tuned to recognize holy things? Jesus said, "My sheep hear my voice" (John 10:27). Do you still hear his voice? Have you become insensitive and deaf to his nearness?

A moving and tragic experience concerns Beethoven, the great composer-musician who went stone-deaf and never heard his own greatest melodies. You can visit his house in Bonn on the Rhine. It is now a museum. One of the most poignant exhibits is a big glass case full of the strangest ear trumpets of all shapes and sizes from one or two inches to three feet or more. With these ear trumpets he tried desperately to hear the music he would never hear again. Equally tragic is the disciple of Christ who no longer can hear the Master's voice. Jesus bids his followers to rest in the quiet place until his voice can be heard. It is then that confidence is restored and strength renewed. It is then that courage is gained for the time and task ahead.

Had the disciples realized what they were to face in the weeks and months to come, they might have broken under the weight of it all. Jesus knew this. He knew they needed to rest awhile for that road ahead would not only be desperately hard but also exhausting to say the least. It would demand the best that was within them plus his added grace.

The experience of that early band of believers is so deeply instructive and helpful for us today. As they faced an uncertain world filled with anxieties, tests and challenges, so we face a similar world. They had no way of knowing what was ahead or where the will of God would lead. Our situation is a kindred one. Thus the admonition of Jesus, "Come rest awhile," is a message meant for our ears as well as theirs. Now the greatest question is whether or not we will listen.

> They came to Him so weary from the journey,
> Depressed of heart for death had claimed a friend;
> What should they do, the fields were white to harvest,
> Then Jesus said, "My friends, Come rest awhile."
>
> How often tried, some child of God in weakness,
> Cries out to blame another for his shame;
> Does he not know, it's meant to be no secret,
> To "rest awhile" will be to live again.
>
> Come learn from God how sacred is the stillness,
> The healing balm that follows quiet prayer;

And precious too, the treasury of promise,
For those who seek will find Him waiting there.

"Come, rest awhile," He softly calls,
"Come, rest awhile."
No day complete without a time with Him,
"Come, rest awhile" Bring every care to Jesus,
Then go refreshed to give your life again.
—"Come, Rest Awhile"

6

The Lesson of the Lake

And straightway he constrained his disciples to get into the ship, and to go to the other side before unto Bethsaida, while he sent away the people.

And when he had sent them away, he departed into a mountain to pray.

And when even was come, the ship was in the midst of the sea, and he alone on the land.

And he saw them toiling in rowing; for the wind was contrary unto them: and about the fourth watch of the night he cometh unto them, walking upon the sea, and would have passed by them.

But when they saw him walking upon the sea, they supposed it had been a spirit, and cried out:

For they all saw him, and were troubled. And immediately he talked with them, and saith unto them, Be of good cheer: it is I; be not afraid.

And he went up unto them into the ship; and the wind ceased: and they were sore amazed in themselves beyond measure, and wondered.

For they considered not the miracle of the loaves: for their heart was hardened.

And when they had passed over, they came into the land of Gennesaret, and drew to the shore. Mark 6:45–53

Jesus had just fed the five thousand with a lunch of a little lad. It was one of those rapturous moments and especially so for his disciples. There was an attitude of stunned wonder as they pondered the miracle wrought by the hands of the young Son of God. No doubt they turned to the ones around them and remarked in exhilaration, "We are followers of the Master. He has called us to walk with him wherever he goes. To us he is Lord and Saviour."

Perhaps that is the reason it came as such a shock to hear Jesus say, "Men, get into the boat and go to the other side of the lake." One can guess their immediate response. "You want us to leave here? Why, we have just witnessed a miracle. This is where holy things are happening. Surely, Lord, you would not ask us to leave now. Surely not just now." But firmly and impressively Jesus said, "Get into the boat and go to the other side of the lake."

No doubt it was with great reluctancy that they boarded the little fishing vessel, pressed out from the shore, and started rowing toward the other side. Little did they know that they were to learn that late evening and night one of the greatest lessons of the Christian life—the lesson of the lake. God had purposed and planned this lake crossing. The divine mind of God knew that they needed the lesson of the lake as much or more than they needed the miracle on the mountain.

The Crisis of Life's Storms

There was a touch of spring in the mid-April air as they began the four-to-seven-mile lake crossing. One would not have guessed that in a brief time the quiet waters of Galilee would be turned into a raging tempest. Storms were not uncommon on the Sea of Galilee, but they were never welcome. Just when the storm broke over their boat we do not know. The next Bible portrait presents the disciples clinging to the boat fearing for their very lives while the wind whipped the sea into a frightening furor. There in the midst of the storm were God's men straining at the oars. This

The Lesson of the Lake

sounds a bit strange, doesn't it? Here were followers of Jesus in the precise place he had instructed them to be. And yet a storm had come that threatened their lives. Had they been disobedient runaways the storm would have been more understandable. But to the contrary, no better men could be found. It is understandably human to question such a circumstance and ask, "What possible good could come out of it?"

Sooner or later all of us are caught in life's storms. There are those times when dreams are shattered, tragedy strikes and hope fades like a barely visible rainbow. Few there are who have not known the buffeting of sorrow's waves and the wet winds of adversity. Where is there one that has not felt the teeth of the storm and longed for the lights of home? It is a false assumption that the will of God leads only into a sea of serenity, when in fact the believer may be directed to board a boat destined for a stormy voyage.

The Reason for the Storm

God who is too wise to make a mistake and too loving to be unkind knew that the disciples could be taught more divine truth in the midst of the storm than by remaining to bask in the light of that mountain miracle. It takes it all, the mountaintop moments and the storm-tossed lake crossings, for God to carve the character of his son into the marble of our lives. That is the reason for the storm. And that is the reason the disciples were in the midst of it. They were led there to learn the lesson of the lake. They must learn that following Christ is more than miracles and mountaintops, more than excited crowds and extra baskets of bread. It is more than flower-strewn pathways and the brush of angel wings. Following Christ includes the sting of disappointment, the walk through the Valley of the Shadow, and the strain of waiting for God's answer while standing on the very edge of all the faith one has. Yes, following Christ must include the lesson of the lake.

There is a beautifully instructive passage in Romans 8 which reads, "And we know that all things work together for good to them that love God, to them who are the called according to his purpose. For whom he did foreknow, he also did predestinate to be conformed to the image of his Son . . ." (Rom. 8:28–29).

God did not say that every event and circumstance is good in itself. Rather he said that those circumstances and events work together for good. What good? For the good of seeing his children conform to the image of his Son. That is what it's all about! All of life with its good and its bad is worked out by the Master Designer to accomplish his purpose and will in the life of the believer.

Seen from this perspective the events and circumstances in the life of the Christian take on new meaning. Whatever those experiences, however difficult, however testing, however full of tears, one thing is certain: each experience has in it purpose and meaning. I do not have to understand it nor know the reason for it. I need only to know that he knows and cares and "doeth all things well."

When I was a lad my walk home from school led by the home of my grandparents. Seldom did I fail to stop for at least a brief visit. Grandmother was a typical "Whistler's Mother" type grandmother. I can never remember seeing her idle. Most often by her side would be stacks of colored material from which she would be cutting little patterns. I would watch with fascination as she pieced together the various colors in symmetry and design. And out of that maze of lovely leftovers would come a beautiful spread or quilt. The years have bleached the color out of many happenings of my childhood, but this memory is etched bright and clear in my mind. Often I have thought of God's great design for

The Lesson of the Lake

our lives. He knows what colors to put together and just what arrangement to bring about and, above all else, how to bring reflections of his Son from the life of every child.

Chosen for Royal Service

If it were left to us we would probably not choose the lake crossing, the storm, nor the waves and wind. I doubt that many of us have prayed to feel the weight of a great burden, the heaviness of pain or the agony of defeat. I doubt if many of us have truly wanted the responsibility for the maimed, the orphan, the unfortunate. And yet for those who have been entrusted and chosen for such royal service, God has multiplied their witness a thousandfold and provided for them a multiplied grace. Robert Browning Hamilton knew this so intimately and wrote in his poem "Along the Road":

> I walked a mile with Pleasure
> She chattered all the way.
> But left me none the wiser
> For all she had to say.
>
> I walked a mile with Sorrow
> And ne'er a word said she;
> But, oh, the things I learned from her
> When Sorrow walked with me!

Some years ago while a student in Southwestern Seminary, I attended a class taught by a magnificent Christian teacher. He was the president of the Seminary. Sometimes on warm spring afternoons when the windows were raised in the classroom there would come a cry across the campus. My teacher's face would cloud and tears would run like little rivers down his face. After a time he would say, "That's my boy. He is a demented lad. He will never be healthy like your children. My wife and I would have chosen to be the parents of a strong and alert child. But God gave to us the stewardship of an unfortunate little boy." And then he would say, "We have thanked God many times for our boy. Because of him we have learned more about God and his blessedness than we would have ever learned had we not been entrusted with his keeping."

I have thought about that glorious man so often. He is in heaven now. I am absolutely sure that one of the reasons he was such a spiritual giant and used to move so many of us nearer to God was because God could trust him with a trouble. God can't trust everybody with a trouble or adversity. But when he finds one in whom he can place such confidence he often uses him to reach an entire community with the message of his sustaining grace.

The storms have a way of teaching us the frailty of human strength. It is only when we come to the end of our own abilities and resources that we discover God's enabling grace. It is when we finally come to rock bottom that we discover the reality of the Rock of Ages!

Life's storms help us to learn the leveling of common sorrow. Could we ever know how to sympathize and understand the burdens, pains and problems of others if we were never called upon to experience them?

The storms have a way of bringing us to a total dependence upon God. When the fury of the tempest breaks we come to recognize that man's capacity, mental acumen, social acceptance, financial independence and human ingenuity, however skilled, are not enough. God pity the man or woman who has no invisible means of support!

Of this one thing I am sure: God will not allow any child of his on any lake in any storm in any boat that will not work out for his spiritual good.

The Lesson of the Lake

Where Is Jesus?

Return with me to that little fishing boat and its fear-filled disciples as they labor against the wind. It is to their everlasting credit that they did not turn back. That would have been the easiest thing to do and perhaps, in the mind of most, the sensible thing to do. But to the disciples the will of their Master was not debatable. Jesus said, "Cross to the other side of the lake." To the other side they would go—at any cost!

It is this kind of faith and dedication that God honors and that the world so desperately needs to see. Their action is a challenge and encouragement to everyone who has ever considered turning back or settling for less than God's perfect will.

There is one final note to this adventure into faith. It has to do with a question the storm-tossed disciples had every right to ask: "Where is Jesus in all of this?" It was a legitimate question, and likely it is one you have asked while facing some impenetrable darkness or bewildering circumstance. Yes, the disciples had every right to ask, "Where is Jesus?" And for their earnest query there was an answer.

Jesus was watching over them. The Word declares, "He saw them toiling in rowing" (v. 48). Whatever else that sentence means, it means that those dedicated disciples were never beyond the sight of the Son of God. Although it was night and the storm was raging, he knew who they were and where they were. What a tremendous word of encouragement! It speaks to us today in whatever circumstance we may find ourselves. He knows who we are and where we are. He knows precisely what it will take to meet our needs.

Jesus was praying for the disciples. Recall the verse, "He departed into a mountain to pray" (v. 46). For whom? For the disciples out in the storm. For what purpose? That they might learn the lesson of the lake. Imagine the power of that prayer. What greater gain could a child of God have than the prayer of the interceding Saviour? A fresh flow of new courage will come to any oarsman laboring against the crosscurrents of life to know that the Christ of Calvary has prayed "Holy Father, keep through thine own name those whom thou hast given me, that they may be one, as we are. . . . I pray not that thou shouldest take them out of the world, but that thou shouldest keep them from the evil" (John 17:11, 15).

Where is Jesus? The Bible says, "He cometh unto them, walking upon the sea . . ." (v. 48). He came to them in their distress walking upon that which they feared would bring about their death. Jesus walked on the water through the storm. Jesus is not a victim of circumstances. He is Lord over circumstances. With his help no problem is unsolvable, no burden is unbearable, no foe undefeatable. Regardless of your situation the God who walks on the water is coming your way.

Where was Jesus? He was near them on the lake calling out to encourage. They heard his voice above the wind and the waves saying, "Be of good cheer: it is I" (v. 50). Have you heard that voice? Has he spoken to you in your storm? If not, perhaps it is because your ears are tuned to the wind instead of the Word. For as surely as "he talked with them" (v. 50), he will talk with you and give to you his word of counsel, comfort and command.

Where was Jesus? The Scripture says, "He went up unto them into the ship" (v. 51). He did not stand at a distance to give advice nor in front of the boat to wave them forward. Rather, he boarded the boat to sail with them in the midst of the storm. This is the most thrilling truth of all—that Jesus comes aboard the boat with us while the storm still rages and, as in that day so in ours, he quiets the angry

The Lesson of the Lake

waves of worry and frustration that break upon our heart.

Where is Jesus? If your heart can contain the joy of one added dimension of truth then read on as this passage so beautifully declares, "And when they had passed over, they came into the land of Gennesaret, and drew to the shore" (v. 53). They were safe on the shore at last. He had brought them safely home. That was like him, you know, to see his children safely home.

Not only were they safe physically, but also these followers of Jesus were stronger spiritually. They were not the same men that left Miracle Mountain. They were better men. They had known the test of the storm and had felt the weariness of the wind. Yes, and they were more committed to Christ than ever before for they had learned what it is to trust their lives into the keeping of the one who walks on the water. They had learned the lesson of the lake.

Thank God the Galilean with his unfathomable grace still walks the troubled sea of mankind, comes to us with his call to new courage, and boards our boat to remain with us until we are safely home.

>Jesus, Saviour, pilot me
>Over life's tempestuous sea;
>Unknown waves before me roll,
>Hiding rock and treach'rous shoal;
>Chart and compass came from Thee:
>Jesus, Saviour, pilot me.
>   —Edward Hopper

7

A Handle to Fit My Hand

Now Peter and John went up together into the temple at the hour of prayer, being the ninth hour.

And a certain man lame from his mother's womb was carried, whom they laid daily at the gate of the temple which is called Beautiful, to ask alms of them that entered into the temple;

Who seeing Peter and John about to go into the temple asked an alms.

And Peter, fastening his eyes upon him with John, said, Look on us.

And he gave heed unto them, expecting to receive something of them.

Then Peter said, Silver and gold have I none; but such as I have give I thee: In the name of Jesus Christ of Nazareth rise up and walk.

And he took him by the right hand, and lifted him up: and immediately his feet and ancle bones received strength.

And he leaping up stood, and walked, and entered with them into the temple, walking, and leaping, and praising God.

And all the people saw him walking and praising God:

And they knew that it was he which sat for alms at the Beautiful gate of the temple: and they were filled with wonder and amazement at that which had happened unto him. Acts 3:1–10

A Handle to Fit My Hand

A national magazine featured an article about a pastor who had experienced mob violence and racial heartbreak in the city where he served. It had opened his eyes. He was convinced that Christians can no longer rest comfortably in the midst of the tremendous evil in the world. They must stand up for what they profess. He himself determined to do what he could to change some of the attitudes in his city, though he did not expect single-handedly to rid the world of evil. Difficult times lay ahead, to be sure. "But if everyone could get hold of the handle that fits his hand, peace on earth could become a reality."

There is a handle that fits your hand and mine. There is a specific work for every child of God to perform. We cannot all do the same thing. We do not all possess the same ability nor talent nor capacity. However, there is a handle—a work—for all of us!

This truth is biblically illustrated in Acts 3 by an experience involving Peter and John. They were on their way to the temple at the hour of prayer. No halo was about their head, no priestly robes called attention to their presence. But in the providence of God they had been chosen for a spiritual assignment.

At the temple gate they heard the cries of a lame man. Each day the beggar had been carried to the temple that he might ask for alms. He had never known the lift of carrying a load for others. He was condemned to be a getter without ever experiencing the privilege of being a giver.

The lame man by the gate is a prime example of humanity outside of Christ, crippled, hopeless, desperately lost. How very often the lame are overlooked. All lameness is not physical; sometimes it is mental or spiritual.

Teach me to care dear Saviour,

> To care until I see
> That as I care for others,
> I learn to live like thee.
> —"Teach Me to Care"

Peter and John heard the cry of the lame man. They had been among those disciples who heard the Master say, "Lift up your eyes, and look on the fields; for they are white already to harvest" (John 4:35). Now the lame man by the gate Beautiful was their "white field" and it made a difference to them. It was like them to care because it was like Jesus to care. It was always like Jesus to care!

Heaven pity the child of God who cannot see "white fields" nor hear lame men cry!

> White fields are more than foreign lands,
> Far more than cultures odd.
> White fields begin where there are men
> Without the Son of God.

Wait! There is much more to consider. It is not enough to know. Knowledge alone is not the answer. It is not enough to hear lame men cry. Hearing alone brooks no favor. It is only enough when care becomes soul deep and fever hot. It is only enough when we do something about the hurt in our brother's heart.

I remember my friend Dr. Cal Guy telling of a home where sickness had left a mother weak and unable to perform the normal housekeeping chores. A neighbor came by and visited for a time. Just before leaving she announced, "If there is anything I can do, just let me know." All around her were needs. There were dishes to be washed, clothes to to be hung up, floors to be swept, dinner to be fixed. But all she could say was, "If there is anything I can do, just let me know." What a tragedy it is to live in a world of needs and never be able to see those needs or to walk in the midst of crippled humanity and broken hearts without ever drying a tear or offering one "cup of cold water."

No one automatically has a concern for others. Genuine care is a commodity hard to come by these days. Theatrical compassion is so unlike the compassion of Christ. O Lord, deliver us from cheap showmanship and professional tears!

Years ago I heard a story that I found unforgettable. In the days when those who attended school had deskmates, a little girl came home to report the death of her deskmate's mother. She was concerned as to how she might sympathize with her friend once she returned to school. Some days later the mother asked, "What did you say to your friend when she returned to school?" The daughter replied, "Oh mother, I didn't say anything. But when she put her head down on the desk and cried I put my head down on the desk and cried with her." This is the definition of care. This is the heart of it. To be like Jesus is to put our head down on the desk and weep with those who weep. It is to be a brother to the broken and a friend to the unwanted and unloved.

Care is always costly. It spells involvement. Care draws the true child of God from the shelter of stained glass. It draws him from the Christian ghetto into the dark corridors of Hate Street and Problem Alley. Care draws him from the comfortable sound of vested choirs into the back roads where brutality and brazen ungodliness breed hell on earth. It leads him there because someone must carry a light and Jesus said, "Ye are the light" (Matt. 5:14).

George McLeod, pioneer of the Iona movement in Scotland, said, "I am recovering the claim that Jesus was not crucified in a cathedral between two candles but on a cross between two thieves on the town garbage heap at the kind of place where synics talk smut and thieves curse and soldiers gamble. Because that is where he died and that is what he died about. And that is where church men should be and that is what churchmanship should be about."

> White fields are more than foreign lands,
> Far more than cultures odd.
> White fields begin where there are men
> Without the Son of God.

Dr. Frank Laubach, whose literacy program has taught more people to read than any program on earth, stood to address a college student body in Kentucky. He stood quietly for the longest time without saying a word. Then with tears flowing he said, "O God, forgive me for ever looking upon my world with dry eyes." Herein is the message of care beautifully illustrated and personalized. What he felt we must feel. His concern must be the concern of our heart. "Lift up your eyes unto the fields," Jesus said, and to look is to see frightened, lonely, broken folk of every color, circumstance and country. To look is to see humanity desperately lost and in need of the Saviour.

Total Commitment to the Task

Peter and John could not be careless and Christlike at the same time. They could not profess to love Jesus and offer no help to the helpless. Therefore, Peter said, "Silver and gold have I none; but such as I have give I thee: In the name of Jesus Christ of Nazareth rise up and walk" (Acts 3:6). Here were men willing to get involved—men who were willing to do what they could and to use what they had.

The language "silver and gold have I none," was not meant to be misunderstood as a confession of inferiority or embarrassment that they had no gold nor silver to give. Rather it meant that they believed that they were in possession of something far more important than silver and gold. They knew Jesus Christ, the giver of life everlasting, and were firmly convinced that his miraculous power was available to work wonders.

There is another truth presented here which we dare not overlook. It is that Peter and John made their talent available to God to use to his glory. What they did we must do. We must give to God the talent, the ability, the gifts he has given to us that he might in turn take those talents and abilities and use them to bind up the broken things of this world.

He wants the doctor and his skills, the carpenter and his tools, the secretary and her typewriter, the decorator and her creativity, the businessman and his intuitiveness, the musician and his artistry. God wants what we have to give. He alone can show us the handle that fits our hand.

Once that handle has been found the truly dedicated follower of Christ must become expendable. Jesus said, "Whosoever will save his life shall lose it; but whosoever shall lose his life for my sake and the gospel's, the same shall save it" (Mark 8:35). When one comes to grips with this great paradox, the work becomes far more important than the worker and there is identity found in the lines of Rudyard Kipling's poem "A Song in Storm":

> How in all time of our distress,
> As in our triumph too,
> The game is more than the player of the game,
> And the ship is more than the crew!

God give us men who are willing to be nothing that Christ can be everything, who are willing to play in the band without insisting on being the director, who will go to the fringe of the world more quickly than they will take the fringe benefits of a glamorous opportunity, who are more dedicated than debonair, more involved than eloquent, more prayerful than poetic, more infilled than frilled.

A Renewed Confidence in Christ

To the lame man by the gate Beautiful, Peter said, "In the name of Jesus Christ of Nazareth rise up and walk" (Acts 3:6). Here is a sight to excite the heart of every angel in heaven! Do you sense the thrill of it, the feel of it? There is no hesitating, no mouthing of probabilities, no banter of worn clichés, no embarrassment or feeling of shame; rather, with a voice sharp and keen Peter said, "In the name of Jesus Christ of Nazareth rise up and walk." Here is faith at its best! Here is confidence that heaven rewards!

There is a desperate need for this kind of confidence. Without it the forces of Christianity are powerless and paralyzed.

Someone rummaging through the records of an old church in New England found this entry in the minutes of the official board:

"A committee was appointed to investigate the squeak in the pulpit." That's no place for a squeak. Nor is there a place in all Christendom for the uncertain sound! The need is for the positive note to be sounded that declares all lame men can be made whole!

Christ Is the Answer

Peter believed that Christ was the answer. To him Jesus was no dead Redeemer nor mere social reformer. He was the Christ, the Son of the Living God. His was no proxy faith, no hollow-ringing emotional jab. His was no stowaway confidence aboard another man's boat. It was the conviction of his very soul that through the power of Jesus of Nazareth that lame man could be made whole. Thus he said, "In the name of Jesus rise up and walk."

A Handle to Fit My Hand

There is the power of it, the weight of it, the wonder of it! Peter believed deeply and everlastingly that Jesus was the answer. Nothing less than this kind of confidence and faith is worthy of the name *Christian*. May God forgive us for so institutionalizing, ritualizing, nationalizing, racializing, localizing, and rationalizing Jesus that we have made him repellent. Let's not try to change him, costume him, or put words in his mouth. Let God be God. Our business, our only business, is to be like Jesus.

Today there is an urgent need for the followers of Christ to be able to say with Peter, "In the name of Jesus Christ of Nazareth rise up and walk." It needs to be said with confidence, with steady and firm deliberateness.

During the early days of World War II an American pilot was shot down over the jungles of Burma. Fortunately he fell into the hands of some friendly Burmese. Soon he was anxious to return to his unit but had no way of returning the many miles without a guide. The path led through seemingly impenetrable forests. As they faced the dense jungle growth the American pilot said, "How can you find the way through this jungle?" The Burmese guide replied, "There is no way. I am the way!"

Peter said to the lame man, "In the name of Jesus Christ of Nazareth rise up and walk." There is no other way. There is no other name. He is the way.

With this Bible experience as our inspiration, let us take up the handle that fits our hand and get on with the Great Commission. To wait may be too late. Let us go now into whatever storm that blows, into whatever path that is right, wherever his will shall lead. Let us do it with dignity, with daring full-orbed faith knowing that we follow one who is more than conqueror.

8

The Unrecognized Christ

And he came to Nazareth, where he had been brought up: and, as his custom was, he went into the synagogue on the sabbath day, and stood up for to read.

And there was delivered unto him the book of the prophet Esaias. And when he had opened the book, he found the place where it was written,

The Spirit of the Lord is upon me, because he hath anointed me to preach the gospel to the poor; he hath sent me to heal the brokenhearted, to preach deliverance to the captives, and recovering of sight to the blind, to set at liberty them that are bruised,

To preach the acceptable year of the Lord.

And he closed the book, and he gave it again to the minister, and sat down. And the eyes of all them that were in the synagogue were fastened on him.

And he began to say unto them, This day is this scripture fulfilled in your ears.

And all bare him witness, and wondered at the gracious words which proceeded out of his mouth. And they said, Is not this Joseph's son?

And he said unto them, Ye will surely say unto me this proverb, Physician, heal thyself: whatsoever we have heard done in Capernaum, do also here in thy country.

And he said, Verily I say unto you, No prophet is accepted in his own country.

But I tell you of a truth, many widows were in Israel in the days of Elias, when the heaven was shut up three years and six months, when great famine was throughout all the land;

The Unrecognized Christ

> But unto none of them was Elias sent, save unto Sarepta, a city of Sidon, unto a woman that was a widow.
>
> And many lepers were in Israel in the time of Eliseus the prophet; and none of them was cleansed, saving Naaman the Syrian.
>
> And all they in the synagogue, when they heard these things, were filled with wrath,
>
> And rose up, and thrust him out of the city, and led him unto the brow of the hill whereon their city was built, that they might cast him down headlong.
>
> But he passing through the midst of them went his way,
>
> And came down to Capernaum, a city of Galilee, and taught them on the sabbath days.
>
> And they were astonished at his doctrine: for his word was with power. Luke 4:16–32

In Alexander Tolstoy's play *The Guest,* Martin, the shoemaker, is informed that the Messiah would visit his shop. He prepared well and waited expectantly for the arrival of the Guest. But apparently the Lord did not come. While waiting he fed a hungry little boy. He gave a glass of water to a thirsty old man and provided clothing for a widow and a little child in need. At day's end the aged pastor came to visit the disappointed Martin and inquired of the day's episodes. Upon hearing Martin's recital he took the Bible and turned to Matthew 25 and said, "Read it, Martin. Read it." It was then the shoemaker read, "For I was an hungred, and ye gave me meat: I was thirsty, and ye gave me drink: I was a stranger, and ye took me in: Naked, and ye clothed me: I was sick, and ye visited me: I was in prison, and ye came unto me.... Verily I say unto you, Inasmuch as ye have done it unto one of the least of these my brethren, ye have done it unto me" (vv. 35–36, 40). The Lord had come in the person of the hungry, thirsty, needy, and had been the "unrecognized Christ."

The day Jesus came to Nazareth was like that. The villagers had spent a lifetime looking for the Messiah. And when he came they did not recognize him! The news of his coming was all over town. In fact, it had spread like a prairie fire over the entire community. Jesus was coming home!

The young Son of God had left his boyhood home months before to begin an itinerant ministry. His fame had spread throughout Galilee. Multitudes had clung to his every word. Recently in Cana (only four miles away) Jesus had performed the startling miracle of turning water to wine. Today he would be in Nazareth. It would be the height of understatement to say the excitement was at fever pitch. The name *Jesus* was upon the lips of everyone. What would he say? What would he do? Where would he go?

Nazareth was not just a lonely little village. It might have appeared so upon first observation. It was nestled in the hill country, actually on the slope of a mountain. Lines of flat-roofed houses stretched against the sky. Terraced gardens, wide-spreading fig trees, graceful palms, scented oranges, silver olive trees and thick hedges were a part of the landscape. All this was framed in rich pasture land.

But Nazareth was more than a little secluded village. Its population at that time was about ten thousand. One of the great caravan routes lay through the village. Men of all nations appeared on the streets of Nazareth at one time or another. It was also one of the great centers of Jewish temple life—a priest center, a place where religion ran deep.

Here Jesus had grown up. He was taught by a deeply religious mother, led to understand the rites of Jewish sonship by his foster father, Joseph, and educated as other children in the village school.

For thirty years he was known as "the carpenter's son." Then there came a day when he left the carpenter shop to show a lost world the way to God.

The Unrecognized Christ

Today Jesus was returning to Nazareth. Perhaps this would be the base of operation for his Galilean ministry. All over the village the words could be heard: Jesus is coming! Jesus is coming! Jesus is coming home today!

The Return

It was the custom in those days to meet a visiting dignitary, rabbi, or important guest at the entrance way of the village. A multitude of well-wishers, kinsmen and curiosity seekers met Jesus and followed him eagerly into Nazareth.

As he turned toward the synagogue the crowd rushed for a place to see and hear their young wonder-worker. Normally a swift pace indicated religious fervor. Today it indicated wide-eyed anticipation of some startling miracle.

The Reception

"As his custom was, he went into the synagogue on the sabbath day" (v. 16). No doubt there were things that offended him, but he went into the synagogue. He knew the hypocrisy, the evil, the envy in the heart of many of the villagers. But he went to the synagogue anyway. We should never let the flaws and failures of others keep us from the Father's house!

The order of service never varied. First came the reading of the law. Next the reading from the prophets. It was at this time the minister brought the scroll to Jesus. He would read the prophetic word and then bring a message to the people.

The Spirit's Unction

He opened the book and began to read. From the beginning there was a difference—it was the anointing of God! Truly he had "returned in the power of the Spirit." He spoke as one sent from God, holy love consumed, inspired.

There is always a difference when one speaks under the anointing of the Holy Spirit. People sense it. They know when God's power is upon a man.

The Demands Upon Our Pastors Today

Dr. Wallace Hamilton, long-time minister of a Methodist church in Florida, said, "The modern preacher has to make as many calls as a country doctor; he has to shake as many hands as a politician. He has to prepare as many briefs as a lawyer. He has to see as many people as a specialist. He has to be as good an executive as a college president. He has to be as good a financier as a banker. And in the midst of it all he has to be so good a diplomat that he can umpire a baseball game between the Knights of Columbus and the Ku Klux Klan."

But all this activity amounts to little, to nothing, if he has no message from the Lord. The only effective ministers are those that speak with the unction of God upon them!

Dangers Our Preachers Face

We have been so anxious to have our ministers fill the role of community leaders and all-around good fellows. We want him to be a part of the service clubs and to chair every neighborhood committee and to be a leader in every civic drive. Then we wonder why little happens in our services. The answer is: he has had little time alone with God. Without God's anointing the only power is the power of the flesh, and that is not enough.

Dr. Floyd Doud Shafer has a good word for our time about our preachers. He says: "Fling him into his office. Tear the office sign from the door and nail the sign, 'Study'. Take him off the mailing list. Lock him up with his books. Force him to be the one man in our community who knows God. Set a time clock on him that would imprison him with thoughts and writings about God for forty hours a week. Shut his mouth from spouting remarks and stop his tongue from always tripping lightly over everything unessential. Bend his knees to the lonesome valley . . . and fire him from the PTA and cancel his country club membership. Rip out his telephone. Burn his ecclesiastical success sheet. Refuse his glad hand. Put water in the gas tank of his community buggy and tell him to be a minister of the Word."

However restless and careless our world appears to be, the people are still hungry to hear a man who has come from his study with the throb of God in his heart ready to bring a message anointed by the Holy Spirit.

The Nature of the Coming Messiah

Jesus spoke that day concerning the nature of the coming Messiah. The Scripture was from Isaiah 61 and read: "The Spirit of the Lord is upon me, because he hath anointed me to preach the gospel to the poor; he hath sent me to heal the brokenhearted, to preach deliverance to the captives, and recovering of sight to the blind, to set at liberty them that are bruised, To preach the acceptable year of the Lord" (Luke 4:18–19). Jesus stopped at a comma. He did not go on in that ancient prophecy of Isaiah which dealt with "the vengeance of God." This was the moment of grace, and his message was a message of amazing grace. He preached of the coming Messiah who would be the friend of the poor in spirit, the physician of the diseased heart, the deliverer of the soul in bondage, the giver of sight to the blind, the mender of that which is broken, the proclaimer of the blessed now. What a message! No one spoke like this man!

It was then that he made the great pronouncement, "This day is this scripture fulfilled" (v. 21). Jesus declared himself to be the long-awaited Messiah, the anointed of the Holy Spirit.

The Rejection

Throughout the synagogue there was a moment of thunderous silence as the weight of his words gripped their very soul. They had heard more than they expected. No one could deny what he read. But for him to announce himself the Messiah was something totally, absolutely and irrevocably unacceptable to one and all! Thus began the dangerous murmuring, "Is not this the carpenter?"

They were perfectly satisfied for him to be the carpenter, even the "builder of miracles"—but the Messiah? Never! He just did not fit the popular concept. True, they were looking for the Messiah and wanted him to come. But they wanted him on their own terms. He must dress the part, act the part, and say what they wanted to hear. Nazareth would have been delighted with a "picture book" Jesus. But when the real Jesus stood up it was more than they could take! They preferred to play games about God—not get involved with God.

> When a blithe infant, lapt in careless joy,
> Sports with a woollen lion—if the toy
> Should come to life, the child, so direly crost,
> Faced with this Actuality were lost. . . .
> Leave us our toys, then; happier we shall stay
> While they remain but toys, and we can play
> With them and do with them as suits us best;
> Reality would add to our unrest. . . .
> We want no living Christ, whose truth intense
> Pretends to no belief in our pretence
> And, flashing on all folly and deceit,
> Would blast our world to ashes at our feet. . . .
> We do but ask to see
> No more of Him below than is displayed
> In the dead plaything our own hands have made

> To lull our fears and comfort us in loss—
> The wooden Christ upon a wooden Cross!
> —St. John Adcock
> "The Divine Tragedy"

They saw him in the light of the customary, the commonplace. Jesus was to them the carpenter's son, nothing more. Theirs was a dull, deadly, familiarity that bred the loss of holy instinctiveness. Thus they did not recognize God when he came to church! He was so near, and yet they missed him.

Why Did They Miss Jesus?

They missed the Master in Nazareth because they were not planning on a divine encounter that day. They came to hear a man, to see a miracle, to have an experience. One cannot help wondering what the average church member expects when he or she comes to church!

They missed the Master because they were not ready for a revolution. The temper of the times needed someone like Jesus. There was a desperate need for revival, reformation, revolution. But they chose to maintain the status quo. They were unwilling to face change. It must be done as it had always been done.

It is dangerous indeed for the people of God to be unwilling to break with the past, unwilling to change with the times, and unwilling to use every modern vehicle of mobility and creativity to get the gospel out to a lost world.

There are some things that never change. Certainly not the message nor the mandate. But the methods and manner of getting that message out must always be subject to change to meet the challenge of new frontiers.

A Look at Our World

We live in a land of 212 million people. Seventy percent

live in urban areas. Eighty million of these people are not members of any religious body. We must reach out to them!

We live in a nation of nomads. The average American moves fourteen times in his lifetime. We minister to a people without roots, always on the move. We must learn to hit a moving target.

There are at least 120 ethnic groups using 85 languages and accounting for almost half of the national population. We must be color blind!

Our youth are struggling desperately because of unstable family life. They are challenged to turn to drugs, alcohol, mystery religions, illicit sex. They face a thousand temptations. We must go before them and lead them to dedicated usefulness in the cause of Christ.

There are four billion internationals that visit our shores every year. This is in itself "missions unlimited."

In Texas alone there are almost four million people (31 percent of the state's population) who are not members of any church. Nearly one out of every three individuals you meet on the street or in your neighborhood never darkens the door of a church.

In this global village where we now live there are 3.7 billion people and 2 billion of them do not know Jesus as Saviour. Investigation shows the world population registers only 8 percent Christian. It is estimated that in ten years that 8 percent will drop to 6 percent. By 2080 the ratio will be down to 2 percent. We are fast going pagan!

This year will end with 50 million more lost people than when it began. Some 146 thousand people will die within the next 24 hours, most of them lost.

Everytime the second hand makes a move on the clock one soul is going out into eternity. And if only 2 percent of the world claims to know Jesus, this means the large majority are going out to meet God without hope.

The Unrecognized Christ

Dr. Kermit Long says, "With all our education, our theology, our fine buildings, our image of the church, we are doing less to win people to Christ than our unschooled forefathers did. We are no longer fishers of men but keepers of the aquarium and we spend most of our time swiping fish from each other's bowl."

Had the villagers of Nazareth received Jesus as Savior that day there would have been a genuine spiritual revolution. The same thing could happen today!

The Price of Following Christ

The reaction of the villagers of Nazareth is recorded. "And all they in the synagogue, when they heard these things, were filled with wrath, And rose up, and thrust him out of the city, and led him unto the brow of the hill whereon their city was built, that they might cast him down headlong" (vv. 28-29). They were unwilling to pay the price to acknowledge and follow Christ.

His friends of Nazareth were filled with wrath, and that wrath boiled up within them in a burst of anger and rage. Their decision was to kill him rather than crown him. The tragedy is they were acting in the name of religion! So many ungodly, unchristian things have been done in the name of Jesus. This is a prime example of just how far mankind will go to have his own way!

Jesus was unacceptable to the world of his day. If Christians have one great thing to fear today it is that we are far too acceptable to the world in which we live. Someone stated recently, "The greatest indictment against Christians today is that no one wants to crucify us."

The Spiritual Atmosphere of Nazareth Was Sterile

There was the hardness of unbelief in that ancient synagogue. And that unbelief harnessed the hands of God. Seldom if ever, do we see a miracle in an atmosphere of unbelief.

A cold, dead worship service is sometimes the pastor's fault, but not always. Sometimes it is the fault of worldly-minded members and cold indifferent Christians who produce an atmosphere that is not conducive to holy happenings. One thing is certain: it is not the fault of God.

The Challenge to the Church

God forgive us should we ever forsake the teaching of the Bible, discount the moral absolutes of God and lose the Spirit of Jesus. Heaven help us not to burn false fire on the altar of God.

From Europe's turmoil of racial and national hatred comes this fable by an unknown writer. A pastor acting under state orders said to his congregation, "All of you who have Jewish fathers will leave and not return." A few worshipers paled and went out. Then the pastor said, "Now, all of you who have Jewish mothers will go out and not return." Again a few people left. Then all who remained turned pale for the figure on the cross above the altar loosened itself and left the sanctuary.

When the Spirit of Jesus leaves our altars and our land, with him goes the Saviour! They missed the Master in Nazareth. He was so close, but they missed him. He can be missed today in cold dead orthodoxy, in ornamentation, in pseudointellectualism, in hyperemotionalism, in the worship of organizations. Yes, he can be missed today.

What Did the Villagers Miss?

It is only fair to ask what the villagers missed by missing Jesus. They missed seeing what God could do. They settled for the manmade. This is one of our problems today. We make plans that occasionally challenge our own resources.

But we seldom, if ever, make plans to challenge the resources of God.

They missed the opportunity of being a part of his great plan and program. There are "times of the Spirit" when God is ready to work a great work. If such times are missed, they seldom come again.

These people missed the opportunity of a personal commitment to Christ. He was in their midst. They could have fallen at his feet. Every individual must decide for himself his own personal relationship to Christ. He dare not let the crowd decide for him.

The Results

It is interesting to note that when Jesus knew he was not wanted, he simply moved through their midst, and went on his way. He is like that. He never stays where he is not wanted. Jesus moved on. If they would not hear him and receive him, he would move on where there were those who would respond. This he did. He went to Capernaum and made it the headquarters of his mighty work. We must never forget that Jesus will get his work done with or without us!

Jesus moves on. It is our business to find out where he is going and be sure we move with him. Not in front of him, not behind him, but with him. Wherever he is going is the way we should go. Whatever the cost let us move with him. And as we go let us take as many to heaven as we can. For that's what it's all about.

> Pass me not, O gentle Saviour,
> Hear my humble cry;
> While on others Thou art calling,
> Do not pass me by.